# CREATING
# SCIENCE FICTION
# COMICS

NIGEL DOBBYN

**PowerKiDS**
press.

NEW YORK

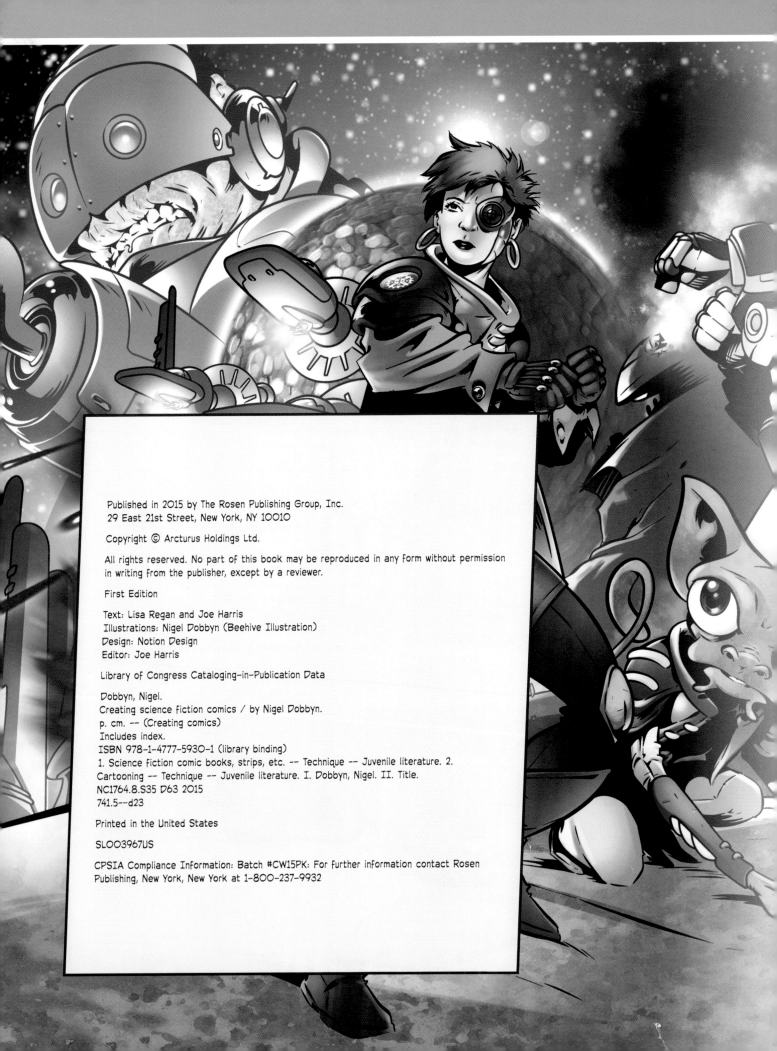

Published in 2015 by The Rosen Publishing Group, Inc.
29 East 21st Street, New York, NY 10010

First Edition

Text: Lisa Regan and Joe Harris
Illustrations: Nigel Dobbyn (Beehive Illustration)
Design: Notion Design
Editor: Joe Harris

Library of Congress Cataloging-in-Publication Data

Dobbyn, Nigel.
Creating science fiction comics / by Nigel Dobbyn.
p. cm. -- (Creating comics)
Includes index.
ISBN 978-1-4777-5930-1 (library binding)
1. Science fiction comic books, strips, etc. -- Technique -- Juvenile literature. 2. Cartooning -- Technique -- Juvenile literature. I. Dobbyn, Nigel. II. Title.
NC1764.8.S35 D63 2015
741.5--d23

Printed in the United States

SL003967US

CPSIA Compliance Information: Batch #CW15PK: For further information contact Rosen Publishing, New York, New York at 1-800-237-9932

# CONTENTS

# TOOLS OF THE TRADE

YOU DON'T NEED EXPENSIVE EQUIPMENT TO START MAKING SCIENCE FICTION COMICS. THE MOST IMPORTANT TOOL IS YOUR OWN IMAGINATION!

## PENCILS

Soft (B, 2B) pencils are great for drawing loosely and are easy to erase. Fine point pencils are handy for adding detail.

## ERASERS

A kneaded eraser molds to shape, so you can use it to remove pencil from tiny areas. Keep a clean, square-edged eraser to hand, too.

## PENS

An artist's pens are his or her most precious tools! Gather a selection with different tips for varying the thickness of your line work.

## FINE LINE AND BRUSH PENS

Fine line pens are excellent for small areas of detail. Brush pens are perfect for varying your line weight or shading large areas.

# PENCILS, INKS, AND COLORS

THERE ARE FOUR STAGES IN THE DRAWING PROCESS. IF YOU FOLLOW THIS METHOD, IT WILL SAVE YOU FROM SPOTTING BASIC MISTAKES WHEN IT IS TOO LATE TO FIX THEM!

## ROUGH SKETCHES

Sketch a "wireframe" first: a basic skeleton of shapes to build your character around. This helps get the proportions and pose right.

## TIGHT SKETCHES

When you are happy with your sketch, it is time to draw over it with firm lines. Then you can erase your rough sketch and add more intricate detail and areas of shading.

## INKS

Use ink to go over all of your final lines. When the ink has dried, erase any pencil marks that are still visible.

## COLORS

You can really let your imagination run wild when you color your creations. Think about how skin, eyes, and hair could differ from what we're used to in daily life.

# DRAWING HUMAN FIGURES

YOUR STORIES MAY BE SET IN OUTER SPACE OR ANOTHER DIMENSION, BUT THEY WILL PROBABLY STILL FEATURE HUMANOID CREATURES. HERE ARE SOME RULES FOR BODY PROPORTIONS THAT YOU CAN USE AS A GUIDE WHEN DRAWING.

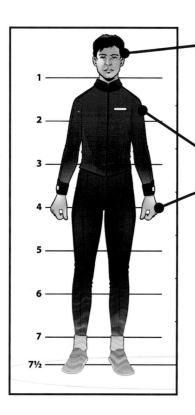

## HEADS
Think of their height in terms of a number of "heads." Males should be between seven and eight heads tall.

## ARMS AND SHOULDERS
The shoulders slope down from the neck into the arms. The hands should sit partway down the thigh when the arms are straightened.

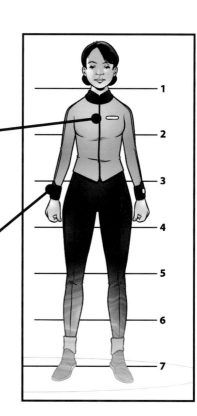

## TORSOS
This female is shorter than the male, so to remain in proportion, her torso is slightly shorter than his.

## LEGS AND HIPS
The female's legs are also shorter (but in proportion). They are slim below the knee, but more shapely at the thigh and hips.

# DRAWING HEADS

THERE ARE NO RULES WITH ALIEN FACES—YOU CAN POSITION THEIR FEATURES WHEREVER YOU LIKE! HOWEVER, YOU WILL NEED SOME PRACTICE FOR DRAWING REALISTIC HUMANS.

## MALE FACE

The eyes should appear about halfway down the head, positioned level with the tops of the ears. Allow an eye-width between the eyes.

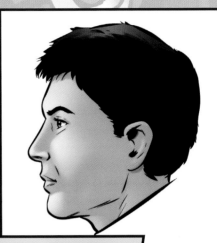

## SIDE VIEW

Male heroes tend to have a square jaw and larger noses than women. Avoid adding too many lines to the face, as they will age your character.

## FEMALE FACE

Notice how the woman's features are smaller and finer. Her eyebrows are thinner, her ears and nose smaller, and her face is more heart-shaped.

## SIDE VIEW

A female character has a rounder jawline. Her lips can take some color. Don't add much color to male lips, or they'll look like they're wearing lipstick.

# A SPACE PIRATE

CAPTAIN XARA QUINN USED TO WORK FOR THE INTERGALACTIC POLICE. HOWEVER, SHE BECAME ANGRY WITH THE CORRUPTION SHE SAW. NOW SHE'S GOING IT ALONE AND KNOWS THERE'S NO SUCH THING AS GOOD GUYS AND BAD GUYS: IT'S EVERY WOMAN FOR HERSELF!

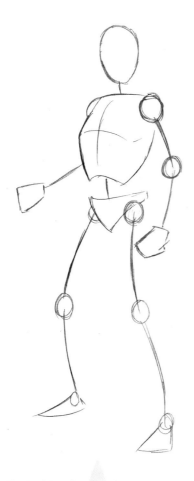

*1* First, you should sketch a wireframe showing how you want Xara to stand. Get the proportions right at this stage.

*2* Flesh out the wireframe with the basic shapes for legs and arms. Add the outline of Xara's military coat and boots. Draw a cross on her face to get the features in the right place.

**3** In true pirate fashion. Xara has an eyepatch—but hers is a futuristic, cybernetic scanner. Sketch her short, funky hair. Add armored shoulder and knee pads and studded gloves. Her hoop earrings are another nod to old-world pirates.

**4** Work up the details of her outfit, such as her utility belt and thigh cuff. Add shadows underneath her coat. A few delicate lines here and there show the folds of her clothes and boots. Finish the features of her face, keeping her tough but feminine.

**5** Now you can begin to go over your final lines with ink. Erase any guide lines that are still visible. Use a fine pen so that you can draw small details, such as her gloves and buttons. She's a funky, punky pirate, and she's ready for action!

**6** Think carefully about your color scheme. Xara's coat and boots are reminiscent of traditional pirates, but her green spiky hair feels modern or even futuristic. Notice how the shading on her coat uses darker tones of the basic colors.

# DRAWING ALIEN CHARACTERS

SCIENCE FICTION IS AN IMAGINATIVE GENRE. YOU WILL NEED TO BE ABLE TO DRAW CREATURES THAT LOOK VERY DIFFERENT FROM THOSE WE MIGHT FIND ON EARTH. WHAT WILL BE YOUR INSPIRATION?

## HUMANOID ALIENS

When you draw a wireframe for a humanoid alien character, consider tweaking and changing the proportions of a normal human. Give them extra limbs, or change the way that their joints work.

SIX EXTRA-LONG ARMS

MULTIPLE EYES LIKE A SPIDER

LEGS WITH TWO KNEE JOINTS

CLOTHING LOOSELY INSPIRED BY THE ANCIENT MIDDLE EAST

As you flesh out the character, think about how the details of their face and body might use features taken from nonhuman animals here on Earth.

You can find inspiration in clothing from different historical periods or parts of the world. Make sure that your character looks the part for their station in life. This creature is an alien queen.

## MONSTROUS ALIENS

When creating an alien monster, it is a good idea to use a combination of Earth creatures as a starting point. This character uses aspects of several creatures, including a wood louse and a crocodile.

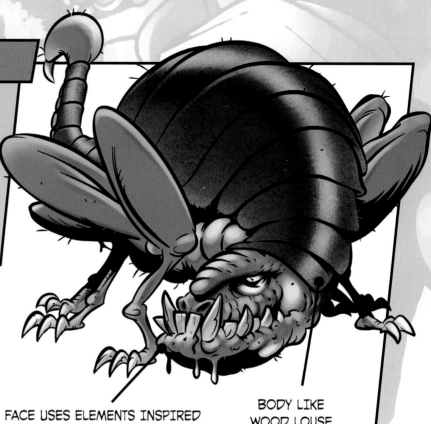

FACE USES ELEMENTS INSPIRED BY CROCODILE AND HIPPO

BODY LIKE WOOD LOUSE AND FROG

## CUTE CRITTERS

If you want a creature to act like an appealing and lovable companion, you will need to follow certain rules. Large heads, big eyes, and rounded body shapes make for cute creatures. Just about everything else is up to you.

PREHENSILE TAIL

LARGE, APELIKE HEAD

# AN ALIEN BIKER

IT MAY LOOK LIKE SOMEONE HAS STOLEN THIS ALIEN BIKER'S WHEELS, BUT THAT'S NO ORDINARY BIKE HE'S RIDING. IT'S A HOVERBIKE! VRILAK SKREE IS THE LEADER OF A FAMOUS SPACE GANG. NO ONE WOULD BE FOOLISH ENOUGH TO STEAL FROM HIM.

*1* Loosely sketch the circles needed for his head, body, and joints. Give Vrilak elongated arms and legs.

*2* When you're happy with his seated position, add the basic shape of his bike. Play around with different shapes to see what looks best. Build up the outline of his limbs and clothes.

**3** Let your imagination run wild when you fill in the details on his bike and outfit. When creating science fiction vehicles, it's a good idea to look at real, present-day vehicles for inspiration. Use the elements that you think look cool.

**4** Think about where the light is coming from and how it will cast shadows. Lit from above, the underside of the bike will be in darkness, with shaded areas where Vrilak's body blocks the light, too. Keep adding more textural details to his outfit. He loves all kinds of studs, chains, and metal plates!

5 Take your time at the inking stage. You don't want to ruin your hard work now that you've come this far. You'll need a steady hand for the curves and circles. Keep the lines on the bike to a minimum, so that Vrilak is still the main focus of attention in the image.

*6* You can have fun choosing strange colors for your alien creatures. Vrilak has green skin like a reptile. The silver and red details of his armor stand out nicely against his black jacket and blue pants. His mohican and his shoulder guards match the bodywork of the bike. What a show-off!

# DRAWING ROBOTS

DRAWING ROBOTS CAN BE DAUNTING. THE IMPORTANT THING TO REMEMBER IS THAT THEY START WITH SIMPLE SHAPES, JUST LIKE DRAWINGS OF PEOPLE. GET THE INITIAL SHAPES RIGHT, AND YOU WILL HAVE A FINISHED ROBOT THAT LOOKS FANTASTIC!

## HUMANOID ROBOT

### BASIC SHAPES
This demolition droid is made up of flattened disks, tubes, cuboids, and egg shapes.

### FINISHED CHARACTER
The fine detail and color transform him! Look out for his heavy-duty blaster arm.

## NONHUMANOID ROBOT

### BASIC SHAPES
This medical droid is not based on any familiar human or animal shapes.

### FINISHED CHARACTER
Add as much detail as you like, from lights and antennae to hatches and grasping hands.

# DRAWING SPACESHIPS

SPACESHIPS CAN BE BIG AND BULKY OR SLEEK AND SLIMLINE. YOU CAN COPY THE BASIC SHAPES OF SHIPS FROM OBJECTS YOU FIND AROUND THE HOUSE, SUCH AS HAIR DRYERS OR KITCHEN APPLIANCES.

## TRANSPORT SHIP

### BASIC SHAPES
This ship is big and bulky, but we have made it narrow at the front.

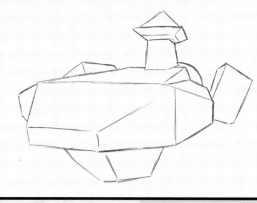

### FINISHED SHIP
The small details on this transport ship, for example, on its tower, give a sense of its size.

## SPACE FIGHTER

### BASIC SHAPES
A fighter ship has a pointed nose and several rocket engines behind.

### FINISHED SHIP
It needs a hatch on top and battalion colors on the nose tip.

# A GIANT MECHA

NO ONE MESSES WITH A MECHA! CREATE YOUR OWN GIANT ROBOT LIKE GIGANAUT HERE, IN THE BEST TRADITION OF JAPANESE SCIENCE FICTION. CONTROLLED BY A HUMAN PILOT, MECHA ARE BIG ENOUGH TO TACKLE GIANT THREATS, SUCH AS DINOSAURLIKE SPACE MONSTERS.

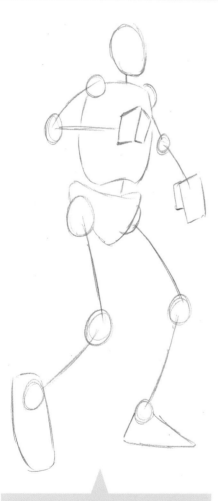

**1** Start with a simple frame. Give your mecha a small head and long legs with huge feet for support.

**2** Build on the frame using basic shapes. Begin to fill out your figure, bulking it up around the shoulders, forearms, and lower legs. Its upper torso should be broad, narrowing at the waist.

3 Sketch in details such as the fingers and rivets, keeping the mechanical feel of your creation. Add straight lines to show the armor plating on the feet and elsewhere. Keep his helmeted head small in comparison to his body.

4 Although he's bulky, Giganaut is agile, and he can run faster than a bullet train. His range of movement is limited by his armor, but the shaded gaps at the knees, waist, elbows, and neck show his flexibility.

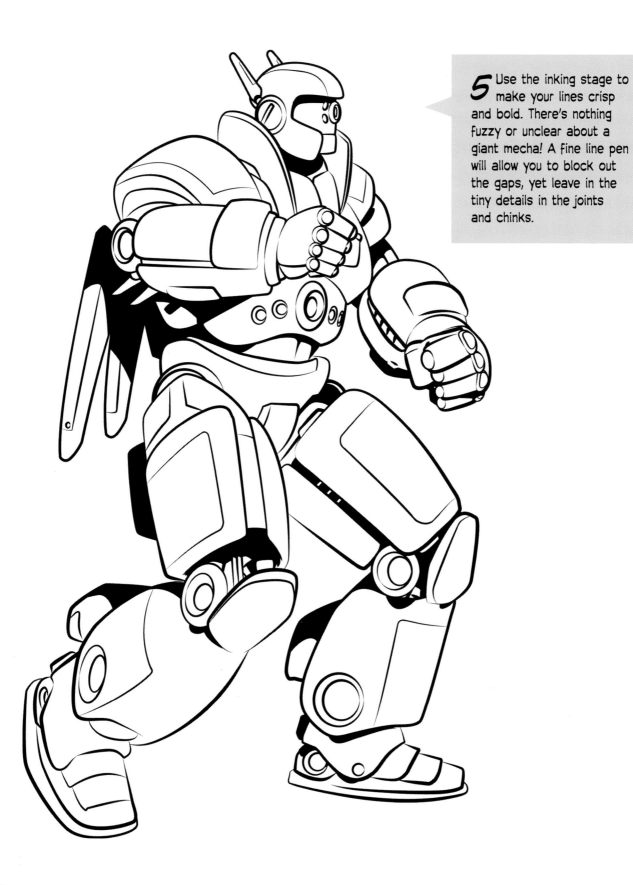

**5** Use the inking stage to make your lines crisp and bold. There's nothing fuzzy or unclear about a giant mecha! A fine line pen will allow you to block out the gaps, yet leave in the tiny details in the joints and chinks.

6 A warrior mecha like Giganaut uses bold colors to show off and frighten the opposition. Add glowing green lights with white and pale highlights, and darker shades of red on his armor to show the shadows.

# DRAWING ALIEN WORLDS

CREATING SCIENCE FICTION CHARACTERS IS FUN, AND INVENTING THE WEIRD WORLDS THEY LIVE IN CAN BE JUST AS REWARDING. BUILD UP A WHOLE UNIVERSE OF WONDERFUL ENVIRONMENTS, BOTH CONSTRUCTED AND NATURAL, AS A SETTING FOR YOUR STORIES.

## ALIEN JUNGLE: PENCIL SKETCH

A good technique for world-building is to mix two real-life elements to make something new. Look at the mushroom tree in the center and the squid plant in the top right-hand corner!

## ALIEN JUNGLE: FINAL IMAGE

The simplest way to make a world look alien is to change the colors and textures of familiar objects. Here we have: yellow soil; a soft-bodied gray tree; purple plant tendrils; and various weird flowers.

## FLYING CITY: PENCIL SKETCH

Sometimes the challenge is not to make something look strange—after all, how often do you see a flying city? With this kind of image, the tricky part is to make the concept feel real and functional.

## FLYING CITY: FINAL IMAGE

Think about how your city works. Make yours a joy to live in with vibrant colors, lots of windows, and greenery amid the streets and buildings. The more industrial elements are hidden out of sight underneath.

# A SCI-FI COMIC COVER

THE COVER OF A COMIC IS ITS MOST IMPORTANT ILLUSTRATION. AFTER ALL, YOU WILL WANT TO MAKE SURE THAT PEOPLE PICK UP YOUR STORY AND READ IT! IF YOU BREAK THE COVER DOWN INTO ITS PARTS, YOU WILL SOON REALIZE THAT IT'S LESS DIFFICULT THAN IT SEEMS AT FIRST.

**1** Start with the wireframe of your central character—we have chosen space pirate Xara. Then fill the rest of the cover with supporting characters. You can use other elements to create drama, as we have done with the spaceship and the giant enemy looming in the background.

2 Now flesh out your characters. Start with the foreground and work back, so that you know how much of any element is hidden by what's in front. Add some rough background detail, such as the building outlines and the billowing smoke cloud.

3 Add more detail to your characters. The mighty mecha, Giganaut, has less detail since he is farther away. Dream up a face for your huge villain. Give the scene some action with a couple of missiles shooting past.

4 When you add ink, be careful not to go overboard. A large scene like this needs less detail on the background items, so that they don't draw attention away from, or clash with, your main characters.

*5* The whole scene is brightly lit from behind by the explosions. Vary the color of large areas, such as the sky. We have left a space at the top for the title of the comic. What will you call your masterpiece?

# GLOSSARY

**CORRUPTION** (cuh-RUHP-shuhn)
Dishonest or illegal behaviour.

**CYBERNETIC** (SY-buhr-NEH-tiks)
Automatically controlled by nerve and brain functions.

**DIMENSION** (dih-MEN-shuhn)
(in science fiction) Another universe that exists separately from our own.

**ELEMENT** (EL-luh-mentz)
A part of something larger or more complex.

**GENRE** (JAHN-ruh)
A category of art or literature.

**HUMANOID** (HYOO-muhn-oyd)
Human-shaped.

**MECHA** (MEK-kah)
A giant robot or machine controlled by people.

**PROPORTIONS**
(pruh-POHR-shuhnz)
The size of body parts in relation to each other.

**REMINISCENT**
(reh-men-ISS-sehnt)
Likely to remind someone of something.

# FURTHER INFORMATION

## FURTHER READING

Carroll, Michael. *How to Draw and Paint Planets, Moons, and Landscapes of Alien Worlds.* New York: Watson-Guptill, 2007.

Marinez, Randy. *Creature Features: Draw Amazing Monsters and Aliens.* Blue Ash, OH: IMPACT Books, 2009.

Pilcher, Tim. *Little Book of Vintage Sci-Fi.* Lewes, UK: ILEX, 2012.

## WEBSITES

Due to the changing nature of internet links, PowerKids Press has developed an online list of sites related to the subject of this book. This site is updated regularly. Please use this link to access the list:

www.powerkidslinks.com/ss/scifi

# INDEX